blunts,
bullets,
and
belligerence

Megan E. Blaising

BOARDHOUSE PUBLISHING

NEW YORK

Published by BoardHouse Publishing, Queens, NY

ISBN: 978-1-7328120-7

BoardHouse Publishing
PO Box 128128
St. Albans, NY 11412

Manufactured in the United States of America

This is dedicated to the fallen soldiers.

Contents

Message to
the Reader

This book is comprised of my more fragile recollections. I experienced each 'gritty' moment, often going toe-to-toe with some of our most neglected and feared citizens. However, it was these delicate moments that forced my most personal and professional growth. It was these moments that reiterated my purpose. This chaos is my sanity. Their trauma is my trauma. Their loss is my loss, and their success is my success.

Names and portions of the conversations have been altered for confidentiality purposes. Furthermore, I encourage cognizance that each occurrence was merely a moment within the lives of those I served. These memories do not summarize my students' lives, but rather their momentary challenges. My goal is to shed light on the vulnerability displayed among students and citizens that are frequently perceived as incapable of grasping the socially constructed ideologies of 'right' and 'wrong.' Everyone alters the concept of *right* to validate their daily decisions. Yet, they harshly judge those living beyond their familiar social parameters. We are generally inclined to fear what we do not understand.

These memories are not to serve as a crusade for social injustices, rather a selfish avenue to remind other social servants, and myself, that the humanistic approach is the most effective and transformative form of care. Humans experience and endure challenges. However, these challenges should not define us. For example, there are people struggling with alcoholism. There are people struggling with sexually maladaptive behaviors. There are people that have committed murder. That said, we experience the same gamut of emotions regardless of the social dimension in which we live. We are connected whether we acknowledge this or not. The difference between those who have traveled down the other side of the fork in the road is their response to perpetuated trauma. Systemic political, social, and educational failures have reinforced a dysfunctional and trauma-focused psychological state allowing for limited development and overall failure to thrive. Question: How can one fully develop and function when living in a constant state of uncertainty and fear? Answer: *They cannot.*

Throughout my academic career, I often questioned the *purpose* of the various curricula I encountered.

These models focused on philosophical 'truths' and theories. I wanted to study the *why* behind our current sociological dynamics. I appreciate theory. However, theories do not provide solutions. Theories are reflective and suggestive, not explanatory. Due to my intrigue and dedication to education reform, I studied the social and psychological effects of discrimination – specifically slavery –on our education system, students and our current societal constructs. These studies guided my approach to the trauma my students withstood. Understanding the intricacies underneath the generationally shared social ideologies allows me to better grasp the source of the behaviors. Thus, allowing me to unfold their perceptions of crisis, specific and probable triggers, and their neurological and psychological navigation of fear and failure. Ultimately, I could address the *why* and not repeatedly address the behavior itself.

Complex social challenges, such as truancy inundate our educational institutions. When my students were absent, I would visit their homes, which were often project housing, shelters, abandoned homes, or trap houses. After I located them, they endured my speech regarding the importance of being present, following-through with your plan, and exposing your family and peers to experiences they have never seen such as graduation or a post-secondary institution. Yet, every time I watched a student walk-out the doors of our school, their next stop was a prison or a grave. I have lost over fifty students, only four deaths to natural causes. Most of my students have been murdered; ninety-nine percent of those students murdered dropped out of school. Lecturing them solely on the importance of education would be unproductive, as our educational system has unremittingly failed my students. Rarely did they feel valued or safe and were more often victims of social promotion – the act of prematurely passing a child to the next grade-level despite not having the adequate skills. I knew that if I could keep my students within our walls, they would feel valued, safe, scholarly, and capable. Keeping my students engaged was no easy task. I lost many battles and many of my students fell victim to homicide, drugs, gangs, sex-trafficking, and prison. They seldom experienced a childhood and were forced to be adults well before their time. I knew in most cases it was only a matter of time before their predetermined life circumstances and toxic environments lured them into the depths of self-contempt –prompting a perpetuated state of self-sabotaging behaviors that could lead to incarceration or death –but never a diploma.

Knocking on the doors of moldy and infested apartments became routine, as did truancy runs occasionally cut short by drug trafficking. One instance I was told a building was "closed for business" by a middle-aged man. Accompanying him were two young boys who were watching intently on the stoop –another child watching from the second-floor window –reminding me of an army of misfits, those disgustingly disregarded by society. I was, and still am, disheartened by the subpar level of guidance and leadership displayed and the lack of desire for younger generations to outperform the last. Yet, I frequently and boldly disrupted 'business,' a bustling and lucrative alternative economy. I attempted to cling to my kids and provide a shed of consistency outside their makeshift gang family and any escape they discovered in the streets. I vividly remember holding distraught, screaming, writhing mothers as they mourned the loss of their children, and feeling that deep, stabbing despair alongside them. I remember holding them and protecting them from seeing their child laying in the street and helping them physically let go of the caskets while they scream out in absolute sorrow. That gut-wrenching wail still haunts me at night. There is nothing more unsettling than this cry. I still feel that knot in the pit of my stomach when my phone rings late at night –fearing that it will be a notification of another life lost, another mother to console and another baby to bury.

I am often asked why I do not have children. My response is, I do. I have thousands. I have thousands to feed, clothe, educate and comfort. The truth is I love them like they are my own, even my over twenty-one-year-old dope boys. Because when I look in their eyes, I see a misunderstood, neglected, love-seeking child that is dying, and will die, for someone to demonstrate the loyalty and devotion they crave and often search for in all the wrong places. Therefore, these deaths are like daggers to my heart; they steal the breath from me. While I escort their mother's down the church aisles to the caskets, hold them up while we lay their child to rest, pray with them and wipe their continuous flow of tears –I hold mine because my strength is necessary for them to remain standing and begin their walk toward some version of peace.

Additionally, I must adhere to my professional creed – *empowering individuals, families, and communities through educational means* –and continue to intentionally serve and diligently protect the thousands of other kids and families from experiencing this same devastation. I have memories of arriving at work just early enough to hear the faint sound of shots fired, which oddly became comforting. I witnessed chaos –blunts, bullets, and belligerence –daily. While I was a witness, my students and families lived it. They are soldiers on a battlefield waging a seemingly endless and ever-evolving war. They are confronted with what feels like an insurmountable challenge –fighting for equality, respect, and peace of mind. My people want to feel wanted, valued, and perhaps more importantly, heard.

Amidst the various tremulous storms a student withstands, their educational institution should serve as their haven. A place they can expect consistency, protection, appreciation, and loyalty. A place that reciprocates the sentiments they so desperately crave –*I am proud of you; you are loved; I appreciate you.* These precious moments strengthen intuitions. I made sure my students had at least one person in their life that looked them in the eye and told them they meant something in this world –they mattered. My students and their families imprinted my conscious with gratitude. I am grateful for the opportunities to serve, the communal respect permitting me to walk alongside them through their private moments, the lessons shared, and the memories created. It is our responsibility as educators to instill this self-assurance and to learn the *why* behind the emotional outbursts, lack of displayed empathy and mere *I don't give a fuck* attitude that can surround our kids like a shield. Until our students feel safe and appreciated, we cannot adequately educate them. If a child does not feel safe, they will not be receptive to the material being presented. Until we begin to take a more holistic approach to education (educating the human being and not just the mind), we will continue to fail our youth. Therefore, I wholeheartedly embrace the culture before curriculum ideology. We must learn to let their trauma be our trauma. Their loss be our loss, and their success be our success. This chaos is my sanity. However, their sanity lies in you.

blunts

tonya

Tonya was a slender, quiet, middle-aged woman who caught my attention during our fall orientation. Her reserved demeanor and balance of silent strength intrigued me. She frequently found her way to my office drowning in self-doubt and uncertainty as she was returning to school after many years and felt overwhelmed. Tonya was re-learning the fundamentals of reading and practicing basic arithmetic as a middle-aged woman. However, the most troubling concern was how timid she acted; she always hid her smile. During one of our lengthier conversations, she divulged that she had been in an extremely abusive marriage and was in the middle of finalizing her divorce. After I expressed empathy for her horrendous experiences, she said, "Don't be sorry Miss Megan. He don't want me. This court hearing will be the easiest thing I've been through yet. He wants to get rid of me as much as I want to erase him from my nightmares." The following days I paid close attention to Tonya by stopping by her classes and scheduling times to check-in. I felt the recent emotional turmoil could impact her in myriad ways, particularly her desire to pursue her academics –and it did. Her attendance declined, she was often tardy, and she was demonstrating significant irritability towards her instructors, particularly when she didn't understand the material. She started giving up when the material became increasingly challenging.

Amidst one of our more light-hearted meetings, Tonya laughed but put a book in front of her mouth to hide her smile. I asked Tonya why she insisted on hiding her smile. She paused and with tears beginning to fill her eyes explained that one of the worst beatings she endured from her husband caused her to lose a few of her teeth. She never had the money to fix them. She described her smile as something she was 'ashamed of' and made her feel 'ugly.'

"Was he a smart man?" I questioned.

Looking somewhat perplexed, she responded, "No, just mean as hell."

I asked her what sense it made to listen to a fool. She laughed and as she did, cupped her hands over her mouth in a child-like fashion. I put my hand on her wrist and guided them down. She continued to smile. I told her she was beautiful. I could tell she had not heard that in a long time.

"Everyone's smile tells their story," I continued. "And your story is powerful." After this conversation, she would stop by just to peek her head around the corner and smile freely. It made my heart happy. She was slowly picking up her pieces.

Yet, Tonya's frustration with reading caused sporadic attendance, tardiness, or early dismissals. Like all of my other students, she knew that if she did not show up for class, I would follow-up. It was late fall, nearing finals and Tonya was absent. I called her on a Thursday, and she explained that she was in the hospital and ill, but would return on Monday. I did not think too much of this as many of our students went to the hospital when they were ill due to the lack of insurance and viable health care options. I told her to be sure she returned on Monday, so we could get back on track and work towards her diploma.

Tonya passed away later that night. She died from complications of Lupus. Her younger cousin timidly came into my office and stood by the side of my desk. Looking down at the floor, she informed me that she passed and inquired about next steps regarding her enrollment. I do not remember what I said after this. However, after she shared this news, it was as if the world around me started moving in slow motion. I remember walking to the faculty restroom, closing the door and leaning up against it, forcing deep, concentrated breaths. My heart hurt –physically hurt. I could not help but let a few tears fall in what felt like reluctant relief as I knew she was finally free. Although, selfishly, I wanted her to experience her freedom here - in this life - because she valiantly worked to lift herself up out of the nadirs of despair and abuse.

This was a beautiful, strong woman who humbly studied with her elementary-aged kids each night. Tonya shared with me that her ex-husband's last words to her were that she was not smart enough to acquire a diploma or beautiful enough to find love. Even with the thorough understanding that untreated trauma often inflicts trauma, the human, impulsive and emotionally drained parts of me was inclined to give him, and anyone else that abused or doubted Tonya, a big "fuck you." Why? Because I am human and I no one else did that for her.

Tonya was intelligent and wise. She was beautiful, loving, and she meant the world to me. She stood up after being beaten down so many times. Tonya was in many ways indestructible. I will never forget her. I went ahead and wrote Tonya's graduation letter as I knew she would eventually graduate –and quite frankly she did. She graduated from a life of abuse and neglect by creating a new life all her own; a life of heartache and pain by continuing to persevere despite what she was told was attainable; a life of fear and uncertainty by enrolling in school and committing to obtain a diploma; a life of frustration and anguish by putting her all into loving her kids the way she craved; a life of hard work and little reward as she lived well below the poverty line and worked two jobs while going to school. Tonya began a new life filled with her dreams, new beginnings, and healing. I knew she would achieve her dream of walking across the stage and receiving her diploma. Tonya left behind three beautiful children and a friend that will always remember her smile and what it represented. I desperately missed her visits just to show me her smile. She was amazing. I will forever remember her humility, grace, and the joy she experienced and expressed for the simple victories.

Dear Tonya,

I am proud of you.
You deserve to feel safe and free.
I encourage you to rediscover yourself,
and share your beautiful smile along the way.
You are loved and appreciated.

fantaisha

Fantaisha was often referred to as a *thug,* but she was more sensitive than most. I saw right through the bold exterior, braided dreads, tattoos, *I don't give a fuck* attitude and incessant smell of marijuana. She was known for selling drugs. However, she was also incredibly charismatic and downright manipulative. Many of my colleagues struggled to see these pervasive qualities as defense mechanisms, rather perceiving them as disrespect. They were not interested to learn *why* she felt the need to protect herself. That said, I came to know Fantaisha quite well. In the beginning, she rebelled by being the quintessential class clown. Once she understood the world kept spinning regardless of how she felt about it, she relaxed and let her guard down. Her next hurdle was chronic absenteeism and truancy. These challenges emerged for various reasons as most truancy cases are complex and never a result of one problem. However, because of several invasive and unorthodox interventions such as calling her home each day she was absent, conducting countless home visits, and on the occasion she was home, bringing her to the school, she entered her senior year. Her graduation was contingent upon her passing the *End Of Course Assessment* (ECA). This was particularly frustrating, as the exam was initially provided during a student's freshman and sophomore year.

We still moved forward with testing preps and college applications. During one of our meetings, Fantaisha became upset when her mother refused to provide her social security number for her FASFA application. Fantaisha said she was "fed up." I asked her to tell me more about why she was so "fed-up." While leaning far back in the chair across from me, staring out the window, Fantaisha shared her frustrations with her mother's excessive drinking, lack of permanency, and hostile and unhealthy living environment, venting, "The walls of my home are bleeding." She explained that the previous renters of the home were dog fighters. In efforts to conceal their operation, the dogs that lost their fights were bound in saran wrap and stored in the walls of the home. Shortly after Fantaisha's family moved in, the walls started feeling soggy and smelled "like bodies."

Fantaisha initially assumed it was a severe case of mold until she went to wipe moisture off a wall and her hand penetrated through, hitting a dog carcass.

She described the stench as being so foul that she became instantly ill. She said her mother laughed at her when she suggested they call the police to report what they found. Her mother frightened her into believing the police would believe they committed this egregious crime. Subsequently, Fantaisha did not report the finding. She waited until her mother passed out from drinking too much and took her little sister to a motel. Her mother never came to look for her. A few weeks later, her mother moved out of the home, and an investigation ensued. There was an unbelievable number of carcasses in the walls of the home. There were even canine body parts in the basement pipes. Evidently, prior to Fantaisha moving in, the house was kept empty –no furniture, just cages. The dogs would fight in the basement, and the clean-up would consist of sweeping the excrement down the main drain then disposing of the bodies in the walls.

A culmination of personal challenges and social inequities caused unnecessary obstacles. Fantaisha did not pass her ECA and therefore could not graduate that spring. We frequently joke that she followed me, as she enrolled at another school I began working in the following semester. Fantaisha graduated the following year, and I was present to witness this milestone, as were her mother and sister. Her mother wreaked of alcohol and was obviously intoxicated. Her clothes and speech were disheveled. The first words Fantaisha's mother said to her daughter post-graduation was, "It's about damn time." She then asked if they could leave as she insisted that she had plans. I remember Fantaisha's face. My heart sank. I tilted her chin up so she was no longer staring at her feet and told her how proud I was of her and how this moment was because of her perseverance and hers alone. Fantaisha looked at me and hugged me and said, "I wouldn't have graduated without you."

I responded, "Yes, you would have. However, these graduation pictures just wouldn't look so good if I weren't in them." We laughed even though I knew she wanted to cry.

Dear Fantasia,

I am proud of you.
You are valuable and visible.
You are loved and appreciated.

deanna

Her presence could not be ignored. Speaking with Deanna was like interacting with a charismatic, older woman. She exuded maturity and wisdom, even at fifteen. Often, she shared funny anecdotes and had a cure for everything –literally. Anytime she heard someone mention an ailment, she quickly rattled off some home-remedy she was certain worked better than any modern medicine. Deanna lived with her grandmother and aunt in a house around the corner from our school, close enough to walk to and from.

The last day before our winter break, Deanna stopped by my office door and asked if she could come in. I invited her to take a seat and asked what I could do for her. She began, "My grandmother always tells me to do things for people, who do things for people. I want to give you something. It took a long time for me to figure out what made the most sense to give you… It had to be important, but I think this works." She reached in her pocket and then stretched out her arm across my desk. She opened her hand and into mine fell a bright blue, square, Mickey Mouse keychain that read 'Florida.' Deanna explained that this was the only gift her mother had given her in all the years she's graced us here on earth. It was important to her; none-theless, she felt like I should have it. Her selflessness amazed me. I was inclined to decline her gift; however, I knew it would be offensive. I thanked her for her generosity and ensured her that I understood the sig-nificance of her sacrifice.

Deanna's mother dropped her on the porch of her grandmother's house when she was a baby and never returned. She was left with nothing but the clothing she was wearing, a blanket and a note that read, "She's better off in your hands." This was the story her grandmother shared with me. Deanna heard from her mother sporadically throughout her life. Every few years, she would send a postcard from a different city. Deanna kept them all in a cardboard box along with the blanket she was wrapped in when she was aban-doned on the front porch. She admitted the postcards inspired her to want to travel. She wanted to, "Help other kids see the world. I don't know just how I'll do that yet, but I will."

One day, she found her mother waiting on the front porch when she arrived home from school. This was the first time she could remember seeing her mother outside of a photograph. When her mother gave the keychain to her, it was wrapped in a Kleenex and presented with a birthday card. Deanna's birthday was in December, and her mother gave her the gift in September; however, Deanna was so excited to be remembered that she didn't care. She described the hug she received from her mother that day like putting on a "nice warm coat in the coldest part of the winter. Your hugs feel like this too... and if you have this keychain, you can't forget me."

"You're unforgettable, Deanna," I assured her, sincerely.

I felt honored to have received this keychain as it was a prized possession. This keychain represented hope and the unconditional love that Deanna craved, yet routinely displayed. She was bestowing these sentiments on me – and for that, I would be forever grateful. I still have this keychain attached to my car keys. It serves as a daily reminder of Deanna's heart and reinforces the ideology that you must give the love you want to receive.

In Deanna's eighth grade year, her grandmother withdrew her to attend a nearby public school. Deanna was quite a bit older than the rest of her peers and had to repeat both sixth and seventh grade during her time with us. By transferring to a nearby public school, she could foray into her age-appropriate grade level. This concerned me due to her inconsistent skill-set; however, I know our school model was no longer serving her. It was a rigorous institution upholding a 'no-tolerance' ideology. Many students were behind despite the nation's infamous, 'No Child Left Behind' tagline. I have not seen or heard from Deanna since she left our school. Still, every time I pass her home, I think of her story and her vivacious personality. Moreover, I am reminded daily of her selflessness and positivity despite her circumstances. She taught me to take time to appreciate the little things, and that *hope* can serve as a lifeline.

Dear Deanna,

You are unforgettable.
You are a light in an often-dark world.
You are loved and appreciated.

mya

I heard a soft voice from my office door ask, "You work here now? I'm Mya." I looked up from my desk filled with an endless mound of files and discipline reports and saw a young girl sheepishly peering around the door sporting one of the sweetest smiles. I introduced myself as I was new to the school. Over the course of the academic year, I learned more about this young lady –her likes, dislikes, fears, and ambitions. She dreamed of being a lawyer because she wanted to advocate for "kids who have been hurt by adults." I also learned that she was a fifteen, nearly sixteen-year-old seventh grader.

As the academic year progressed, students treated her poorly. They often ostracized her because of her age and attacked her intellect. Eventually, Mya started evading class and would hide in the restroom. She would sit in a locked stall on the toilet, arms wrapped around her legs in hopes that no one would find her. When other administrators would notify me of her absence, I would find her and sit with her. She would cry as I consoled her.

The school had high academic expectations. They perceived excellence as a standard and collected numerous accolades to support this. Nevertheless, the model lacked appropriate emotional and behavioral supports. Students were filtered out merely on partialities –and fast. While our administration unapologetically adhered to the philosophy of not permitting students to the next grade level until all the necessary skills were gained and standardized testing requirements were satisfied, the support services to facilitate these requirements were minimal. This allowed the institution to cater to a specific demographic without being required to advertise this practice publicly. Pursuing cultural and academic excellence is necessary. However, the frustration with this design is that many students are being neglected that could succeed and need this structure, in some cases, more than those beneficiaries. There are kids like Mya who have endured significant amounts of emotional, physical, and sexual abuse and others that are regularly subjected to chaos upon leaving the school, which disrupts the implementation of this educational model. Kids that are in desperate need, however, are forced out due to the lack of accessible, appropriate supports would propel them towards a path of excellence. They are thus denied an opportunity to fight for a spot on the post-secondary playing field and beyond.

When Mya discovered she would repeat the seventh grade for the third time, her mother withdrew her. I vividly remember when Mya walked out of our school doors for the last time. It was a warm spring afternoon with bright blue, clear skies. I watched her walk out with all her school supplies bundled in her arms. As she marched down the main corridor, she stopped and pivoted towards the trash can and threw everything away before turning back towards me. She hugged me tight and said, "I love you, mama."

I returned the sentiment. "Love you too, baby girl."

The following academic year, she enrolled at one of the local public schools. She forayed into her *age-appropriate* grade level but was not academically prepared. Subsequently, she stopped attending regularly.

The next time I saw Mya's sweet smile, it was on the news. Her mother was sharing a photo of Mya to the media, hoping to solicit leads in finding the person responsible for murdering her daughter. I was standing in my living room when I saw the picture of Mya appear on the screen. I remember the news anchor declaring, "Another deadly shooting" and thinking, she's not just 'another' anything. She's Mya. She's human. Not a number... Not a number. Sadly, that's not how America views her, and others killed by violence. They are conditioned to believe that somehow their deaths are lesser than those deaths by other causes. Somehow, those that die by violence are less human.

Mya was found in a car with a gunshot wound to the head. She was with another young lady –also a former student. I saw this, and my chest tightened. I closed my eyes, fell to my knees, and I prayed. I asked God to embrace her in his loving arms and let her feel the unconditional love she craved; to let her see herself through his eyes, her mere wondrousness. The pain I felt would not let me cry. It barely let me breathe. She deserved better. I could no longer console her. I believe my challenge was knowing that she was alone during her final breaths –that no one was there to wipe her tears, tell her she was brave and beautiful or be there to hold her hand while God placed it in his own to take her home. Mya's spirit was genuine. When I close my eyes, I can still hear her soft voice. I see and feel her tears. I feel her hugs and, most importantly, I see her sweet smile.

Dear Mya,

I am proud of you.
You are scholarly.
You are beautiful.
You are loved and appreciated.

randall

Randall was a caring and sensitive seventh grader who typically seemed more 'in-tune' than his peers. He demonstrated a significant amount of compassion for his younger brother Travis, a sixth grader. I would watch Randall fix Travis's collar each morning before they would enter the cafeteria. Randall and Travis would sit at a table by themselves near the stage and read. While they interacted with peers, they more often stayed to themselves. Still, they happily greeted me each time I saw them.

One Friday morning, Randall appeared to be more tired than normal, and Travis was not with him. Per usual, I asked how he was doing, and he sleepily replied, "I'm alright, Miss Megan." After he picked up his breakfast tray at the counter in the cafeteria, he sat quietly at a table by himself near the stage. The cafeteria served as a multipurpose room. We often hosted guest speakers and held student-related events in this space. After he quietly ate his breakfast, I asked him to take a walk with me. He obliged. We started walking the halls of the school slowly. We were halfway down the middle school corridor when Randall stopped and leaned his head on his forearm against a locker. He was silent but was visibly upset and started to cry. I leaned my back against lockers next to him. He turned away from me slightly.

"What's going on Randall?"

He replied, with his face now in his elbow, "Can I cuss?"

I had to smile, because God only knew what was going to fly out of his mouth, but told him that if he was frustrated, I wanted him to be able to express it how he felt most comfortable. He abruptly said, "I'm fucking tired. I am tired of not sleeping and being a parent. Miss Megan, I want to be a kid and do kid shit."

While I was somewhat relieved at what I was hearing – provided his inquiry for permission to cuss –I was also deeply saddened yet moved by his level of awareness. "What do you mean?" I gently prompted.

"Every night, my brother and I sleep in the closet of our bedroom because people shoot outside, and the bullets come through our house. My brother isn't here because his pants had a bullet hole in it. My mom didn't want to send him to school because she is afraid we would get in trouble. Miss Megan, those pants were hanging over us in the closet last night. This shit gets so old... it makes me want to go out there and shoot back. The people shooting don't get it. Nobody gets it... It sounds like we live in a war." By this point, he mirrored me with his back against the lockers. Tears stained his cheeks. He continued, "I tried to make sleeping in a closet a game for Travis by telling him we were making a fortress, but he knows this isn't for fun anymore. He's afraid, and I stay up because he wakes up screaming sometimes and it scares me." He wipes his face with his shirt. My heart hurts for him, his family, and the community. I understand how, like many of my students, the last thing on his mind would be school. Randall admitted, "This place is where I come to get away. I know what to expect here, and it is not flying bullets."

I was glad he felt secure at school. Many students in our greater school system cannot say that. I was grateful we could provide a sense of stability in a world so uncertain. I gave him a hug and checked on him a few times that day. I wanted him to know that he was heard and valued. I went to the store in which we purchased our uniforms and provided him a pair to give his brother in efforts to keep him from missing any more school. I told Randall, "You both deserve to feel safe. These are for your brother. You don't have to tell anyone where you got them, just that we had extra at the school. If you need to come early or stay later, you tell me, and we will make arrangements."

He smiled and said, "Thanks for looking out."

I responded, "Always. Keep your head up."

Randall and his brother withdrew from our school a year later and I have not heard from them since. However, every time I drive by his street, I think of him and his brother curled up in the closet. It nearly brings tears to my eyes. They are being conditioned to live in fear. This fear is fostering resentment, which, if left unaddressed, will only manifest into something more significant. Their environment is debilitating. It is stifling the development of their youth. It is impacting their general functionality, but ultimately, their ability to thrive. At thirteen years old, he has learned more about the psychological impact of poverty than most. He understood he was playing the role of an adult at age thirteen. He desperately wanted to do "kid shit." I wanted that for him. He cannot play outside like many of his peers. His decision to play outside could result in a choice between surviving or death –an ultimatum too many of our youth encounter.

Dear Randall,

You are a drafted soldier fighting a war
that should not exist.
You are wise beyond your years
and stronger than your fears.
You are loved and appreciated.

bullets

tony

Indianapolis is notorious for horrendous potholes during the winter months and this year was no exception. I was at an east side gas station, angrily filling one of my tires while determining how I would explain to the city the level of unacceptability that every road arrogantly displayed when I heard a man calling my name.

"Miss Megan?" I stand up and see a tall, middle-aged man cautiously walking toward me. He introduces himself. "My name is Brother Malachi. You may not remember me because we did not get a chance to talk at my nephew's funeral." His nephew was Tony, a former student of mine, he wanted to thank me for what I did that day. At this moment, I had no recollection of what he could be referring to and was beginning to wonder if he was confusing me with someone else. He continued to describe the moment as if he was reliving it vividly, and as he spoke, I joined him on this emotional experience.

Tony's grandfather, younger brother, and mother were sitting in the first pew to the right of the casket. I sat alongside them during the service. I remember the smell of his mother's perfume and the feeling of her warm tears occasionally falling and hitting my hand as I held hers while a member of the church choir sang a beautiful rendition of the hymn, *His Eye is on the Sparrow.* Tony's grandfather was to be one of the pallbearers. However, when it came time for this transition, his grandfather did not move. He just stared straight ahead, towards the altar. It was as if there was no one else in the sanctuary –just him, his thoughts, and God. Tony's younger brother jumped up to take his place and carried Tony's casket down the central aisle. As he was walking, he continued to grow more emotional. I could see the tears streaming down his face and falling onto his new suit jacket. I saw him physically shaking and clenching his jaw, trying to hold it together. His emotions caused both him and the casket to buckle. The procession paused. He avidly tried to regain his grip. As this transpired, I looked at his mother, and shifted her hand to her lap. I stood up, walked over to the casket, and slid in to take his place. As he placed the casket on my shoulder, I took his hand in mine, and we proceeded down the aisle side by side. At this moment the congregation stood in honor of Tony. I believe his brother cried because not only did he lose his brother and best friend, he also assumed new responsibilities, such as serving as the head of the household —all at the age of fourteen years old. After the burial, the family met at Tony's grandmother's home for a meal. While I was standing in the kitchen getting ready to take Tony's mother a plate, Tony's grandfather slowly walked up to me using his wooden cane and in silence looked at me with weary eyes and gave me a hug. He then went out to the back porch and sat with their bulldog, Stanley, for the duration of the gathering.

I was blown away by this detailed recollection and that he remembered me. Tony's uncle shifted from his intense emotional memory to inquire about my personal life, including my ex-husband. I informed him that I was divorced. Immediately he responded, "He feared greatness. He was weak. You need someone who will carry your casket, your burdens, and walk alongside you like you did for my nephew —not because you can't, but because that's what you do and what you deserve." At this moment, I was certain that God sent this man to share this message with me. He wished me well and reminded me to make sure I did not settle for anyone not strong enough to carry my casket to its resting place no matter the distance.

My car ride home was filled with memories of Tony. They played through my mind like a short film. I remember Tony would eat nothing green and feared the dark even at eighteen years old. He had a charming and distinct smile, the product of a diagonal chip in his front right tooth. In elementary school, while playing ball with his friends on a local outdoor court, an elbow rammed into his face. The fight that ensued gave him the chipped tooth, but he never could afford to fix it. I remembered the at-length conversations about his fears, but more so, his ambitions. I knew he secretly perceived his gang affiliation as both a job and a source of survival. His favorite candy was strawberry flavored pop-rocks. He loved superhero movies because he admired how they could secretly transform into "someone else and no one knew it was them. Someone that did a lot of good for a lot of folks." I remember his cry when he talked about his younger sister who was killed by a drunk driver while they were both outside playing in the spring of 2013. Moreover, I remember the night he was murdered.

The fear, franticness, and uncertainty in Tony's cousin's voice were apparent when he called to tell me he wasn't sure if it was Tony laying in the street. I was often called by family members during a crisis, an indication of the solid relationships I built. The nature of my job was to assist with sensitive needs, such as significant impoverishment, therapeutic needs, and crisis-related issues. There was a trust that was established. In this particular case, Tony's cousin was also a student at the time. After speaking with his cousin, I rushed to the location. I do not even remember the drive there. I was so focused on how I needed to address this and what potential challenges could arise. I parked about a block away from the caution tapes. I saw people starting to gather around the perimeter. As I approached, I saw a stray Nike shoe, laces undone. I kept walking. A little further down, I saw his hand that laid outstretched, palm-up. He was face-up on the blacktop just a few houses down from his home under the infamous white sheet. The uncertainty and fear I heard in his cousin's voice were solidified when I saw the pink and white beads that were tied at the end of his cornrows. These were his sister's beads. He wore them in honor of her.

His mother, who worked a night shift, drove up. Before the car stopped, she jumped out and ran over towards the crime scene. Trying to pull down the tape, I grabbed hold of her and pulled her back. She knew. I knew. She screamed out in utter agony as if she was experiencing the six bullets that pierced her son in the chest. I held her while she sobbed and continued to stare at those pink and white beads. I badly wanted to hold him and remind him that he was loved and appreciated. I wanted to tell him that while he lay there directly under a streetlight, it was not how he would be remembered. He is more than a statistic. He is Tony, and he has a story. For all intents and purposes, he is a kid. I think about his love for superheroes and how he is now transformed. He can rest assured that his legacy and memory has "did a lot of good for a lot of folks." People now know Tony. Just like my other students, there is a sincere fragility and an intricate story behind the media's general erroneous portrayal and those God-forsaken white sheets.

Dear Tony,

Never forget that one man can change the world.
You are loved and appreciated.

juwan

Beyond the block, attending school was one of Juwan's daily afflictions. That said, I still built and maintained a relationship with this twenty-year-old young man. During my several home visits to encourage him to attend and engage in school, I met his daughter and his grandmother. I even built relationships with folks from around-the-way, those young and old. Some people were earning their stripes, others just hustled and there were 'old-heads,' a term referring to people who have been in the dope-game for a long time. Sadly, today, the term 'old-heads' refers to someone still alive and hustling in their mid-20's. They all knew him and agreed he should pursue his diploma. However, these were the same people that introduced him to this lifestyle –this captivity. During conversations, internal conflict was rampant. There was a dire need to explain their lifestyle was not something they wanted for Juwan, and how they were sure that if they had acquired their high school diploma, their life would have been drastically different. That said, when they saw him, those conversations faded into oblivion, and the game with no real win or end continued.

It was mid-morning. I had just finished hall sweeps to ensure students were in class and not loitering. I stopped by the main office to collect my mail. While I was emptying my mailbox, an administrator stopped me to tell me that Juwan walked out of his credit recovery class and wanted to speak with me. I walked towards my office and found him sitting in one of the chairs with his head tilted back against the wall, wearing a somber look. It was evident that something was bothering him. Frequently, like so many of my students, Juwan flirted with the temptations of the street. For my students, this flirtation often involved one of three circumstances; being forced to live in a chaotic environment and watch their surroundings like an uncut version of the HBO series *The Wire*, indulging in this lucrative –yet dissociative –hustle and generating more money than some of our administrators, or hustling when necessary. The commonality is they were all inevitably traumatized.

I walked up to him, smiled a little, and said, "Walk with me."

We exchanged small-talk on the way mostly about the weather as it was finally getting warm out. He told me he liked to be outside. He liked to "smell the fresh air... makes me feel free." We made our way to the library and sat at one of the vacant tables. I asked him how I could best support him. He explained he had been attending this school for his entire high school career, and not one teacher *wanted* him to be there. He believed no one wanted him to truly succeed. They always passed him on to the next grade –practicing social promotion. This is a common practice within our public-school system –an unyielding contributing factor to our ill-equipped graduates, inaccurate and still unacceptably low graduation rates and other poor-educational representations. If instructors no longer want to 'deal' with a student or feel they are getting 'too old' for their current grade they simply allow them to foray into the next grade level without the necessary skills. Students that are socially promoted are often described as *over aged and under credited* and often land in these credit recovery courses.

Juwan stared off towards the window for a minute, clenched his jaw then looked directly at me with watery eyes. He turned to his left, pointed to a book on the shelf entitled *When You Give a Mouse a Cookie.* He paused, trying to gather himself, before revealing, "I can't even tell you what that says. What do I look like coming to school each day staring at a computer screen that I can't even read? I come to school to get torn apart. I can't even read to my daughter. No one helped me, they just passed me on to get me out. Here I am twenty-years-old, and I can't fucking read."

I was in emotional shock. I felt Juwan's feelings were legitimate and was furious at the miscarriage we referred to as our education system. With nothing to utter of intellectual value, I simply pulled my chair around, put my hand on his shoulder, and let him cry. He was a grown man, crying in the library of a high school –deemed illiterate by state standards –that could have potentially been provided a waiver to graduate in a traditional public school. They would have knowingly permitted him to be unequipped to navigate and thrive in society. I felt helpless. Yet it wasn't too late for Juwan. Our institution just did not have the proper programming to support his needs, and I knew our administration would not try to change that either. The city does not have much for this demographic –and the programs we have are not effective as there is no follow-up. We fail this group daily and then complain about unemployment, imprisonment and recidivism rates, etc. Sometimes our ignorance makes me laugh because we are our problem. We are our own worst enemy. We simply are too lazy to address these issues. Unfortunately, we are prideful and do not want to admit that we are flawed and have been since our conception.

We discussed his character and strength. I needed him to know people noticed his positive qualities as he had many. I remember the moment when I looked at him and told him he was a good person. He was nearly unable to accept or believe the compliment, but I pursued eye contact and insisted, "I appreciate you." He let a few tears fall and gave me a hug. He also signed out of school that day.

A short while later, I walked into the Registrar's office while Juwan was attempting to complete the withdrawal form. Persuaded by what I assume was embarrassment, he asked me not to watch him. I ignored his request and sat down next to him, watching as he stared blankly at the sheet. Still not looking at me, he asked where he should start. We went through each portion of the document, but even with my assistance, he struggled. He could not even accurately spell the name of his street. Finally, we arrived at the last portion, which required a signature. When he was unable to sign his name, he got frustrated, scribbled something and threw the clipboard into the wall. The Registrar was startled and stood, ready to call the Dean. I put my hand up, indicating she should not and got her to sit and hold-off on any disciplinary action. I walked out of the office and watched Juwan walk down the hall and out of the main doors. While I understood his rationale, my heart still broke a little that day because he believed he failed. That will never be alright.

I never saw Juwan again. I received a voicemail a couple of weeks later that said, "This is Juwan. [Silence]. I'm sorry. I know I'll see you around the way. You're everywhere... Saving the world, one thug at a time. Don't stop. [Silence]. I appreciate you."

Dear Juwan,

I am proud of you.
You are capable of greatness.
You are loved and appreciated.

kenyiah

Kenyiah had a small group of friends but primarily remained to herself. She did not get in trouble at school and performed at the top of her class. She had dreams of attending a four-year university. Specifically, an Ivy League because she wanted to 'disrupt statistics' –I liked that. I was intrigued by the degree of intentionality and ambition she demonstrated at only fifteen years old. That said, I desperately wished she could enjoy being a child, even though I do not recall ever working with a student who had this luxury. Frequently, Kenyiah would stay after school and work on her English homework at a table in my office until her mom could pick her up.

Our school building was older, so it was either too hot or too cold –rarely was it comfortable. On this day, it was rather hot. I could tell that Kenyiah was uncomfortably warm, but she chose not to remove her sweatshirt. I offered her a hair tie from my resource closet. She gladly took it and tied up her hair but repositioned her chair so that her back was facing the wall farthest from me.

"Everything okay?" I asked, noting her behavior.

She glanced at me uneasily and answered, "Yes."

I said, "Alright," and continued organizing boxes of donations graciously provided by a local church. Another administrator stopped by my office and offered us bottled water –we obliged. A few moments later, Kenyiah accidentally dropped her bottle –spilling it on the table and floor. She jumped up in a panic and began profusely apologizing. This frantic behavior was not new to me as I have encountered many students that have been victims of abuse and provide immediate fear-based responses. I assured her she was alright; she was not in trouble; it was an accident; I am not upset, and she was safe. She started tearing up because her sweatshirt was wet, and she did not want her mom to see and be upset with her. I asked Kenyiah to remove it so I could put it in the dryer before she arrived to pick her up. She declined immediately. I encouraged her to think about this while we cleaned up and we could talk about it again afterward.

As I walked over to throw away the paper towels, we used to wipe up the water, she said, "Miss Megan, do you trust me?"

"You haven't given me a reason not to."

When I turned towards her, she observed, "I'm like a wishing well. People look at me and see this unique entity they can cast their hopes and dreams upon, but really I am stone cold with deep dark secrets… and if I let you inside, you will see nothing but darkness. If I invite you in, you'll fall until you hit rock bottom. That's where my heart lies."

I was simultaneously enthralled and devastated by her meticulous self-reflection, and I wanted to learn more. She asked me to close my eyes. I did. When I was asked to open them, she was standing before me with her arms stretched out in front of her and her sweat-shirt was removed. Her arms were covered in burns. They were nearly multicolored –so much so it was as if patches of skin were missing. It appeared she had no hair on her arms.

She said, "This is what my entire body looks like."

Kenyiah explained that her biological father battled heroin addiction and, "One day, he was high…really high, and he started burning me with the spoon he used to shoot up. When I started crying, he picked me up and put me in the oven that I guess my mama left on. She was supposed to be making something but fell asleep. My mama said she could 'smell me cooking' and that is what woke her up. It was the smell of my burning flesh." In addition to the gruesome story, she said something that I will never forget. "The devil may have marked me; however, God has my heart in his hands." There is no greater truth than this.

I gazed at her in wonderment, telling her, "Your scars are the testimonies of your heart, the heart that God holds firmly in his hands." She looked back down at her arms with despondency. I reached out and placed my hands on her forearms. "These are your victories thus far. You are more than a 'stone cold wishing well for others...' you are an abyss of greatness. Let these serve as a reminder of what you can survive." She hugged me and cried. I cried with her... for her. She asked how anyone would think this is beautiful. I responded, "Because you do."

She smiled and stated, "I like that." I dried her sweatshirt and got her a new bottle of water.

I often reflect on Kenyiah and her story. Not because of the horrendous actions of her father, but because of the survivor she is and how the complexities of our psyche' can permit us to believe we are anything less than beautiful and remarkable because of someone else's inadequacies. Kenyiah transferred to another school in the next academic year, and my professional endeavors lead me elsewhere. Unfortunately, I have not remained in contact with her. However, she's always in my thoughts. I think of her scars and what they represent as it forces me to look at mine and remember what I can and have survived. I think of her courage to stand before me with such humility and reveal her deepest, darkest moments that have beautifully tattooed her body. She helps me regain my strength as I remind myself, "The devil may have marked me; however, God has my heart in his hands." I pray she finds bliss in her beauty and an abundance of strength in her story.

Dear Kenyiah,

You are an abyss of greatness.
You define beauty.
When someone points at your scars,
remember who holds your heart.
You are loved and appreciated.

donte

The mere intangibility that Donte felt when he considered his educational path seemed insuperable. He thought he would never make it off the 'hamster wheel' that he was riding since grade school. He was nineteen years old and classified a freshman. His academic capabilities had not really improved since the second grade mainly due to poverty, lack of proper academic supports, and early exposure to the harsh realities of a world riddled with shortcomings and empty promises. It was time for Donte's annual case conference, meaning that any service providers he may work with, school administrators and his teacher of record meet with him and a parent to discuss his academic progress, reevaluate and update his individualized education plan or IEP. The meeting convened and his teacher of record and the special education staff discussed his shortcomings –his significant amount of missing work, spotty attendance, and recent display of aggressive behaviors towards another male student. After a few moments of listening to my colleagues, I tuned them out and watched Donte's face. He looked overwhelmed –not by stress, but by the labels silently attached to him. I immediately interjected and started identifying his growth by maintaining regular contact with me and keeping all our required appointments. Moreover, I witnessed him being more sociable with his peers and staff and saw him take an interest in learning, even if it was for short stints of time. I suggested we start getting creative with our educational approach and less cynical. Focusing on what he is not doing is not going to inspire this adult male to come back to high school each day and do the work he knows he is supposed to have already completed at this point.

I instantly became unpopular, but I didn't care. I cared for the tender spirit that still resided within Donte. I needed him not to forfeit. Understand that Donte was a part of a notorious gang, had a two-year-old daughter, and desperately clung to any job he could acquire, trying not to make his living as he always had before – hustling. He lived a gritty-ass life outside these doors, so I was doing everything I could to make him feel safe, welcomed, inspired, and worthwhile during his time with us. However, like all my kids, Donte needed this diploma.

After my interjection, I asked him what he wanted to get out of this academic year as I wanted to hear directly from him what would mean enough to him to get up each morning, be present and engaged in the learning process. He stared me dead in my eyes and said, "Miss Megan, I just want to be able to read books to my daughter. I want her to be smart. I don't want my mama to have to help me make out the words in front of her. I want my daughter to know she can ask me how to say a word when she doesn't know how. I want her to feel smart and powerful."

His mother rubbed his back gently in comfort. I maintained eye contact with him and replied, "Well, all right, Donte. You have yourself a deal. You want to be able to read to your daughter by June 9th; you are going to be able to read to your daughter by June 9th."

Eventually, everyone else virtually gave up on the meeting, realizing that nothing else mattered to him, or me for that matter, and we excused ourselves and went to the school library. He picked out a few children's books that he thought his daughter would like: Clifford the Big Red Dog, Good Night Moon, and a few others. We created a schedule of three times a week to work on his reading. It was March when his case conference occurred. Know that by June 9th, that young man read an entire Clifford the Big Red Dog book with no assistance. It was the first time I saw the child so deeply buried, linger in his deep brown and weary eyes. I was unpopular for some time. That was fine. I did not have the wherewithal to concern myself with popularity and feelings bound by nonsensical practice. I was here to ensure that my students had an advocate and more importantly left our school with skills that would serve them in the world in which they lived, even if they left prematurely. Quite frankly, Donte's goals were no different from the administrations. We needed him to improve his reading ability, attendance rate, and overall engagement, and all those things occurred – just by allowing him to feel heard and valued.

I later addressed the team with these sentiments, adding that we must be mindful of two things. First, encouraging significant consideration to the mind space in which our youth are coming to us. We must meet them where they are and accommodate each learning style because they live lives with demands many of us could not imagine. Second, feelings are messy. Particularly, when it comes to business. If you find yourself feeling a particular way, I encourage you to ask yourself if it is an adult problem or a student problem and act accordingly. Because nine times out of ten, it will be an adult problem –meaning you need to reevaluate how you are approaching the matter at hand. It's time to get creative –and they did.

I have physically removed Donte from fights, placed my hands over the fresh cuts he gouged in his wrist to stop the bleeding during a suicide attempt, supported him through his stay at a local psychiatric hospital for his suicidal ideation, held his mother while she wept in the corridors of the school because they had nowhere to live, and ultimately watched him withdraw. However, Donte went on to graduate from Job Corps. His journey was tumultuous and triumphant. I will never forget the day that he sent me a picture of his diploma and a message that read 'Thank you for keeping me in school.' Donte is a prime example of a child born into the unjust jungle of impoverishment and yet was expected to survive in an institution that does not support the survival mentality. I still speak with Donte and his mother. He has a full-time job as a brick mason as he received his certification while at Job Corps. He now has another child, and I receive pictures regularly. In fact, I received one this summer of him reading a book to his kids. My heart was happy because I knew he was finally happy too.

Dear Donte,

You are worthy of being heard.
You are extraordinary.
You are loved and appreciated.

belligerence

jasmine

"I need ten stacks, or you are not going to see this bitch again. Matter of a fact, make it forty –her cute-ass can make me a lot of money."

I was listening to a sex-trafficker on speaker phone in the presence of a missing-persons' detective and Jasmine, my student. He kidnapped her younger sister after she exited a city bus two weeks prior. The detective and I were providing prompts or inquiries for her to use in efforts to gain information regarding their location. A few days later they located her sister, a few other young girls –ages fourteen to seventeen –and the few men connected to the crime in a motel on the far-eastside of the city. The men were charged with a plethora of crimes, including multiple counts of kidnapping, rape, and sex-trafficking.

It was not the family's first encounter with sexual predators. The girls were targeted before. While they had not been kidnapped and forced to have sex with multiple people for weeks with little food or water, they resided in a prime area for trafficking and trading. Jasmine was a young lady with a timid disposition and a mature physique which garnered unsolicited attention from males. She survived multiple violent sexual assaults prompting emotional outbursts, disappearances and general rebellions. Consequently, Jasmine did not attend school regularly and experimented with drugs, causing her to fall dramatically behind in school.

When she enrolled at my school, she began therapy and endured a steady course load. She appeared to manage this relatively well –until her sister was kidnapped. This disrupted the significant progress she had been making with both myself and her Home-Based Therapist. Ultimately, she stopped attending and ran away from home. I never heard from her again. However, I frequently consider how, as an institution, we could have provided more solid support services to inundate our students' social-emotional needs. I heard she was spotted in various locations notorious for sex-trafficking. I frequently reminisce upon that conversation– listening to him making demands as if he had the right; as if she wasn't human or someone's daughter, sister, or granddaughter. It was as if she didn't matter at all. I remember how badly I wanted to veer from what was vehemently necessary to acquire information to locate and keep her sister alive and tell him what I really felt. However, I listened for cues and breaks of confidence in his voice and continued to write questions for Jasmine to ask to keep him on the phone.

Typically, when people hear the word slavery, it prompts an immediate disregard to whatever message follows, as society has been conditioned to fall victim to their initial emotive response rather than wholly embracing and deconstructing this concept. Ironically, this term looms in the shadows of our country's foundation, as if the existence of slavery is somehow debatable. Slavery is rarely discussed in our educational institutions, media outlets, and it's for damn sure not discussed around our dinner tables. However, sex-trafficking, this new-age form of bondage, still facilitates prosperity. A similar slavery-like philosophical practice induces and projects comparable residual and multifarious psychological traumas over entire populations. Thus, reinforcing the ideology that there are significant and inhibiting psychological effects caused by oppressive and discriminatory practices.

Dear Jasmine,

I am proud of you.
You are worth fighting for.
You are loved and appreciated.

janae'

Janae' arrived at my office with a pink hall pass in hand and a note that read, 'black eye, won't talk.' I asked Janae' to have a seat at one of the chairs in my office. I pulled up a chair and sat next to her. As I examined her, I noticed the entire right side of her face was black and blue. I initiated a conversation, inquiring whether she understood why she had been asked to come down to my office. While still holding a blank expression on her face, she motioned her head to indicate 'yes.' I asked her if I could look at her face. Her silence was incredibly uncharacteristic. Typically, Janae' was outgoing and known for her robust laugh. It was distinct and often got her noticed by her teachers during the worst times. It was for this reason, Janae' and I got to know one another well. She was frequently sent to my office for 'redirection.' Quite frankly, she was funny. It was difficult to remain serious when she was sharing her version of what brought her to my door.

After Janae' indicated I could look at her face, I began to realize how extensive her bruising was. It ventured down the right side of her neck and ended just before her collar bone and extended back into her hairline from approximately the middle of her forehead. While I was reviewing her injuries, she was looking at the floor.

"What happened?" I asked, tracing her injuries with my eyes. She continued to be silent. "Janae, what happened?" Tears were running down her cheeks and falling onto her shirt like rain, yet she remained silent. I handed her a box of tissues and resumed sitting next to her. Janae's crying became physically overwhelming. I encouraged her to breathe saying, "Come on, baby, I need you to breathe." I walked through what that looked like. We took some deep breaths together. She began to calm down enough to catch her breath.

Once she regained some control, she blurted, "I can't do this anymore." Another long silence and then, "My mama has been beating us since I can remember, and as I get older, it gets worse." Janae' had two other sisters –one older who also attended our school and one younger that attended a nearby elementary school. "My mama tells me all the time that I look just like my father." Janae' turned toward me desperately, relaying how she tried to stay "out the way" –as if she was trying to convince me –but nothing stopped the fighting. Her mother and her boyfriend would drink, seek the three children out, provoke them, then beat them.

The night before, Janae took their alcohol bottles outside and threw them over the fence into the adjacent alley. "I was mad and tired of their bullshit. All they do is drink, get high, bitch, argue and fight us… it's tiring. I'm tired. I'm so tired. I'm here at school, and my life's different. I can be what I want. When I'm home, it's like I have to fight just to live… literally… I am growing to hate them, but I also feel bad for her. My father left us. One day he just never came home from work. It was really hard. I hated him for it because we had to sleep in our car for a while and a couple of shelters, but more than that my mama has been fucked up ever since. She started drinking a lot. My daddy was dark-skinned like me…" Putting her head down and holding back tears, she whispered, "I think my mama thinks she can beat him out of me so she can get rid of all reminders of him." Out of all the demoralizing things that Janae' was sharing with me, this was the most heart-breaking. Overcoming physical abuse even at various developmental stages is exceptionally challenging, however, to untangle the intricate web of psychological damage bestowed on this beautiful soul was devastating.

Imagine how this young girl is internalizing this message –I am not good enough; I am not beautiful; I am not an individual; I represent something hurtful. I am not your daughter and everything beautiful that should be, but rather a representation of a hurtful memory you selfishly and unhealthily nurture. With tears in my eyes, I grab ahold of her hand. We sit for a few moments. I pray silently. I put my arm around her shoulder and draw her close as she cries. I just hold her and rub her hair when she puts her head on my shoulder.

I expressed my concern for her ongoing safety in the home. Moreover, legal obligations had to be considered now that I was aware of what happened to her and her siblings. I explained the next steps and how I would be there during each of them while at school.

She responded, "I'm ready. I'm scared but ready. I can't live there. I don't know what my sisters will say or do, but I can't do it anymore."

The police started their interviews and examinations, including photos. I met with Janae's sister and initiated that process. Her response was similar –she was tired and relieved that the abuse was no longer a secret. Hours later, the preliminary investigation was complete, and a caseworker was ready to take them to a foster home. It was at this point the girls became frantic. Janae' stood up, backed into a corner, and started crying. I could console her some, expressing how important each stage of the process was. As the caseworker was attempting to guide them out of the office and ultimately out of the building, Janae' latched on to me, hugging me tight with her arms around my shoulders.

She started crying and yelling loudly, "Please adopt me. You can be my mama. Let me live with you. I promise I will be good. I clean up. I listen. I swear, I will. Please... Please. I don't want to go with them. I don't know them." The caseworker was now attempting to pull her arms off me, and I tell her to be brave, and I know she is good, but she was still screaming, "Please, Miss Megan. I will be good –just let me come with you. I don't want to go with them." I tell the caseworker to hold off;

however, she has called an officer, and Janae's sister was growing upset. Repeatedly, I advised both of them to calm down, not resist and promise we would talk soon but was eventually asked to leave the room. I told the officer and case manager, again, to wait because the girls were not emotionally ready, and no one was trying to help them get there. They physically escort me out because all I could focus on was making sure Janae heard that she was strong, and everything was going to be okay. She needed it. Hell- maybe I needed it.

To my surprise, after weeks of no contact, their foster mother brought them to the school to visit me and introduce herself. They were attending another school due to where they now resided, however, they were safe. I had a lengthy conversation with the foster mother. I reminded her that each of the girls was loved deeply. She understood. I still see her from time to time around the neighborhood as she has fostered several of my students over the years. When she sees me, she always says, "Don't worry Miss Megan, I'm loving the babies."

I have not seen them since but think of them often. Specifically, Janae' and whether I failed her. I think about how different her life could have been if I did let her and her sisters live with me. I am glad that she was no longer being abused. She no longer had these bullshit messages drilled into her psyche. I miss her laugh and her smile. If I could tell her anything, I would want her to know that her smile puts an even bigger one on my face and to remember she means something in this world.

Dear Janae',

You are beautiful.
Your soul is stunning.
Your bravery is unmatched.
You are loved and appreciated.

kierra

Kierra was a quiet, intelligent, and poised young lady. She usually came by my office to check-in and talk through her revised post-graduation goals and arrived promptly and prepared daily. She wanted to attend a four-year university to become a veterinarian.

One particular day, Kierra stopped by my office, and I immediately noticed that something was on her mind. She was stoic and looked frightened. I inquired about what was bothering her. She stared at me as if she had so much to say but could not get the words to come out. After she took a seat, I shut the office door and sat in a chair beside her. While staring out the window, she asked, "Miss Megan, is there anything I could tell you that would change your perception of me?"

I assured her that there was nothing she could do or say that would alter how I perceived her. "We are human, which naturally makes us imperfect; and because of this, we are to demonstrate grace and mercy."

There were a few charged moments of Kierra looking at me then down at her feet before words began to pour out of her. "I feel like I have failed you and anyone who believed in me. I definitely failed myself… Miss Megan, I am pregnant."

I would be lying to say I was not taken aback only because I knew that her road instantly became more challenging regardless of her decision moving forward. Despite my surprise, I said, "You being pregnant does not change my perception of you at all."

Kierra smiled at me sadly, then confessed, "My mom is making me get an abortion." Kierra started crying. Everything was happening so fast that it was hard for her to know what she wanted. However, she did feel it was unfair for her mother to make a decision for her. Kierra and her mother did not have a great relationship. Her mother jumped from boyfriend to boyfriend, and Kierra often felt neglected. I had met six of her mother's boyfriends in the two years I worked for this institution. This should provide some perspective, provided my interaction with parents was not as frequent as the students. After a little while of being in my office, processing her situation, Kierra decided she was ready to return to class. I escorted her to her last period.

The next day, Kierra did not show up to school. I thought she went forth and scheduled a consultation for her abortion. I called her home when we did not receive an absent notification from her mother but received no response. Kierra did not show up the next day either; however, this time, her mother left a message on the attendance line indicating that Kierra was ill and would be out of school. Kierra finally returned to school the following day. She stopped by my office but was once again quiet. My office was packed with scholars attempting to gain passes to class, so I told her I would come check-in with her as soon as I cleared everyone out. After I cleared the hallways, I stopped by her homeroom. The teacher said Kierra never showed up to class. I did a radio check and discovered she was not in sight of any staff. Finally, I checked one of our girl's restrooms, and there she was, sitting on the floor with blood-stained pants.

I immediately checked her vitals and pulled the radio to call for emergency assistance. Kierra begged for me to wait. She pleaded for me to wait for one moment and, reluctantly, I paused to hear her out. Her vitals were normal; however, she was readily bleeding. "You have seconds to tell me what you need to tell me, Kierra. You need medical attention."

Kierra gasped in pain. "Please just sit with me. I am losing the baby and I don't want to lose it alone... please don't bring in an audience... just be with me. My mom made me take the pills and said I had to go to school, so I didn't bleed in her house." Her sobs were becoming violent. I wet paper towels and placed them on her head. I lean her back against me holding her hand and encouraging her to breathe. I remind her that everything is going to be alright and that she is strong. Nevertheless, the nurse and her mother needed to be called as we could not knowingly allow her to have an abortion at school. But I promised to keep her condition as 'low-profile' as I could. I called the nurse from my cell phone and asked she bring towels explaining there was an emergency.

The nurse arrived and looked panicked when she saw the blood stain visibly expanding on Kierra's pants and restroom floor. In an effort to shield Kierra from the other woman's unease, I instructed the nurse to bring me the towels and immediately start explaining that Kierra took prescribed abortion pills, and this was the result. I maneuvered Kierra into the wheelchair the nurse brought with her by putting my arms under hers and lifting her up into the seat. When Kierra was situated, I stepped outside of the restroom and called our principal to share an update and then called Kierra's mother.

It took every ounce of strength I had not to allow my personal feelings to convolute my professional obligations while speaking with her mother. She did not seem to understand the problem with her completing this process at school. Kierra's mother arrived sometime later. I indicated that Kierra was unable to return to school without a doctor's note. Also, we needed to have a parent conference before she walked back into a classroom. I helped put Kierra into the car. I then went back to the restroom to get the towels and clean up the mess that was left behind. I turned to wet some paper towels, looked up into the mirror and realized I had blood on my pants and the bottom of my shirt. Instantly, emptiness filled the pit of my stomach. I started scrubbing as hard as I could. I found myself growing angry... pissed. I wanted to rip the fucking sink off the wall. Quite frankly, I wanted to destroy that whole fucking bathroom. I stopped, slid down the wall, and sat with my head tilted back against it. I closed my eyes and just sat there. I did not want to open them because I could not stand to see the mess or the blood-stained footprints. It would make this real.

I had other kids to tend to and knew I needed to gather myself quickly. Following a deep breath, I stood up to finish cleaning up the residual. When this task was completed, I walked into the principal's office. Before I could even say a word and he shook his head "No, you need to be walking to your car. You must take care of yourself."

I felt dazed, and like I failed. I went home, showered vigorously, and found myself replaying the series of events and what Kierra said to me, "…just be with me…" I wondered if she felt I was there for her. I briefly wondered if someone would ever be there for me. In a moment of selfishness, I recalled the tragedies I witnessed during that year alone and felt like I wanted someone to "…just be with me…" Then I reminded myself that my comfort comes from being there for others. My hand is held when I hold theirs. I am held when I hold them. I closed my eyes and remembered what I told her, "You are strong... Everything is going to be alright." I don't think people fully understand the fucked up shit that social workers and counselors hear and witness in a day's work. Yes, every school experiences the challenges that spawn from the jungle-like roots of poverty on some level. However, for those schools that disenfranchised communities are bound to, crisis is often a constant state of being. I am not complaining because I loved my career with every fiber of my being. I am taking this opportunity to shed light on the invisible psychological bridge that exists between two worlds and how we -myself and fellow social servants- walk this path balancing our own mental health needs unbeknownst to most.

Kierra and her mother returned to school that following Monday. The principal, Kierra, myself and her mother met in the main conference room to discuss the series of events and the plan moving forward. Her mother stated she did not fully understand the gravity of the situation until after the fact. Moreover, she did not want her at the house during this process and did not know where else to send her. She said, "I didn't know it was going to be more than a little spotting."

I leaned back in my chair. "Ma'am, with all due respect, you sent your child to school knowing she was in the process of having an abortion. I do not give a shit how much bleeding you thought was going to take place. She was losing a child. You did not want her at her home, so you sent her to be alone while losing a human being. Forgive my language, but that shit is inexcusable." The principal reached towards my arm, indicating I should probably stop while I was ahead.

Her mother leaned forward in agitation. "I really feel some type of way –like you are trying to judge me. I'm a single mother…"

I pulled away from the principal's hand and interrupted what I felt was going to be another piss-poor excuse. "Yes, you are the parent. I cannot tell you how to raise your child; however, I can tell you that mess you pulled will haunt her for the rest of her life and for that you should feel 'some type of way'." She sat quietly and just glared at me. I glanced over at Kierra who had tears on her face but was steadily staring at the floor. The principal looked like he was unsure of what was to follow. I stood up, excused myself, and walked out. In full transparency, I did not feel that bad. I was mad, felt Kierra's mother was living in a foolish fairy tale, and I was going to hold her accountable. Yet the more I thought about it, the less I was able to determine to whose standards I was holding her to. I know the intricacies of trauma well, but who was I to judge her decisions? She was operating within the context she knew best. I called her later that day to apologize for my behavior in the conference room.

She said, "Miss Megan, I need her to learn to hurt on her own. I need to know she'll be okay if she is left to herself." I acknowledged and respected the ideal she was attempting to instill and chose to forfeit this battle.

Kierra finished strong at our school and was accepted to a handful of universities. I watched her walk across our stage and acquire her diploma. Her mother brought a new boyfriend to her ceremony. That said, Kierra told me their relationship improved some after that tragedy. It was not a monumental improvement; however, an improvement nonetheless, and she welcomed it with open arms, just as I welcomed her in mine for the last time on the day of her graduation. She gave me a card that had a note nicely folded inside. It expressed her gratitude for my support and encouragement, but most touchingly, it read, "Thank u for making me see my strength." What Kierra does not know is that she reminded me of mine.

Dear Kierra,

I admire your unrivaled courage.
You are loved and appreciated.

dedra

Dedra commanded attention when she entered a room –not because she was boisterous, but because she was gorgeous. She sheepishly wore a natural beauty most desired. I became familiar with Dedra because she was frequently tardy to school. One day, she stopped in my office and asked me if I would be willing to meet with her regularly. I agreed.

The day of our first session, she appeared timidly in the doorway. I invited her in, and we sat at the table in my office. She began by stating, "I don't know how to talk, but I know if I don't do it, I will become a version of myself that I don't want to live with. Miss Megan, I feel alone and like I don't belong anywhere. Until about a year ago, I lived with my father because my mother was incarcerated for a convenience store robbery and attempted murder… she's been in since I was eight years old. My father and I did not have a great relationship." Dedra paused heavily. "If I go on, I just need to know you aren't going to look at me different."

I reassured her there was nothing she could tell me that would cause me to view her differently as I already had seen her heart. She smiled and said, "You are the only person that can see hearts when everyone else just sees our circumstance."

Smiling, I replied, "It is not difficult when you know that everyone has one, and it was all created by one source."

Dedra became quiet and gazed out the window. I could see her eyes filling with tears. I handed her tissue, and she let the tears fall down her cheeks. With some effort, she met my eyes. "I have been having sex with my dad and his friends since right before my ninth birthday. I am gross, and my heart is dirty," she agonized, clenching the tissue between her fist. "He started coming into my room at night, and things escalated over time. Later on, he would have friends over, and they would do the same thing. I felt like a business deal. I have been infected with Chlamydia numerous times and have a Pelvic Inflammatory Disease. I had a miscarriage when I was thirteen...thirteen... and I don't even know who the father was... probably my own." I felt like I had been hit in the stomach. I was disgusted by the actions of her father and his friends – not solely for the acts themselves, but for the lasting impact they would have on her psyche. Women already have numerous psychological barriers to overcome as society readily dictates our acceptable role(s) and media outlets advertise our *ideal* image.

Dedra continued, "I walk around feeling dirty every day, and since he's been locked up, I still don't feel better. He used to tell me that I was old enough to decide if I wanted to have sex with him or not, and I believed it. I felt like I had to, and I did, or he would always threaten to put me out –at eight, that was scary. I had nowhere else to go." She said her father would have 'poker nights' and whoever won first had 'first-dibs' on her. At this point, I felt physically ill. I could see she did too. She was viciously tearing at the tissue in her hands and laying it out meticulously on her legs. "I just want to feel as beautiful as everyone tells me that I am because right now I hate the way I look. I hate that people look at me. I sometimes close my eyes and pretend I live on a pretty, warm island like Jamaica and no one can get to me… but then I open my eyes and realize I am still stuck in this life I hate. This life I didn't want." She turned to me and said, "You are confident; yet, I can see the pain in your eyes. People with pain, see the pain in others. That is why I came to you. I don't know what you have been through, but I pray it will allow you to help me."

I was impressed by her perceptiveness and candor. I would support her and help her find a new version of peace, as she deserved nothing less than to feel like, "the powerful and beautiful young lady you are." I will never forget her response. She looked at me in my eyes and promised, "And I will be there for you..."

Dedra was perceptive. She was honest and desperate for someone to provide the assurance she was missing her entire life. Her grandmother moved to Indiana from Missouri after she was removed from her father's care. She resided with her while attending our school. We worked diligently on self-image, self-care, self-appreciation, and 'acceptance of what is.' Perhaps most importantly, we worked on deconstructing our conditioning to blame ourselves for the shortcomings and poor behaviors of others. Dedra started to accept and practice these lessons, understanding that her father's disgusting decisions did not define her and/or limit who she can become. Quite frankly, we both did.

During one meeting, I took her into the girl's restroom and stood her in front of a full-length mirror. She instantly pulled away. I guided her back. I reminded her, "We're in this together." She closed her eyes, breathed deeply, and opened them to peer into the mirror. I asked her to identify three things she liked about her physical person.

"I hate my lips; I hate my hips; I hate it all –they loved it, so I hate it."

"Today we are starting over," I announced. "No one defines you, but you." She asked me what I liked about myself. I responded, "My smile because it is my armor –it attempts to hide my pain from the world; my eyes because if you stare into them long enough you will see the mountains and valleys I have traveled to stand before you, and my skin because it tells my family's history."

Dedra came back to my office the following day and closed the door behind her. She said, "I love my eyes today… because I can look into them and see the little girl, I feared was dead, is still living. I saw her today. I saw her when I remembered you standing side by side with me in the mirror." Dedra and I continued to work with one another throughout the year. I watched her blossom before me and it was incredible. Dedra withdrew from our school the following year; however, I still get updates from her cousin, who also attended our school. Dedra will never know how she impacted my life. She forced me to pay attention to my pain. I pass her grandmother's home daily as it is on my route to work. I smile and remember that I have my shield. I hope she still wears her smile too –like armor.

Dear Dedra,

Your heart is beautiful.
I pray you find your version of peace.
I pray you continue to wear your smile
like the shield of a warrior.
You are loved and appreciated.

josiah

I am greeted in the main office by Josiah, a student, an officer, and a Guidance Counselor first thing on a Monday morning. Josiah had his hands rolled up under his shirt. I escorted them to my office and asked how I could help. Josiah pulled his hands out, revealing them to be bloody from human bite marks. Additionally, he had burn marks on his forearms. I put on gloves and began my examination while acquiring information about how the injuries were sustained.

"I made breakfast this morning and spilled the box of cereal on the floor. I knocked it over when I reached for milk. My mama got upset because she said I did a shitty job cleaning up. I didn't get up all the cereal, and she bit me for every piece I missed. And the burn marks are from her cigarettes because she said I started crying like a little bitch." He shrugged, "It doesn't hurt now, though." Josiah divulged that his mom often bit him as a form of discipline because, "he was slow, and this is what books say to do when slow people act up."

I took him to the nurse and had her treat his wounds. The next stop was with the Special Education Department to begin the process of filing a report. I sat with

Josiah during his treatment and interviews. He was worried that his mother would be mad at him. More so, he was worried that he would 'mess-up' and do something else that warranted punishment. Josiah had a mild form of Autism and other cognitive challenges. His mother later reported that she was taught to respond like this to his behaviors. Sometimes when Josiah would get really upset, he would bite others, so she believed she was to reiterate his behavior.

Josiah had a tender soul. He was self-conscious, however, worked diligently to be accepted among his peers. This meant a lot to him. Sometimes this desire would get him in trouble in class, but he wanted to be normal so people did not treat him differently or laugh at him. His desire to 'be normal' – whatever *normal* actually is – saddened me. He was such a kind-hearted young man with grave sensitivities towards others. He always offered a helping hand and jokes when he thought someone was sad. His presence made you smile. Once I transitioned to another school, I did not hear or speak to Josiah again. Even so, every time I encounter someone longing to 'fit-in,' or I hear a trivial one-liner joke, my mind goes to him. I pray for his safety and hope that he will accept himself as is. I want him to be bound by nothing –no preconceived notion that he is less than any peer. He is not defined by his diagnoses; and above all, I hope he knows that he is loved and appreciated.

Dear Josiah,

Be bound by nothing.
You are capable of greatness.
You are loved and appreciated.

To all who discredit....

To all who discredit, overlook or inaccurately perceive my students:

You are perpetuating the cycle of poverty.

You are reiterating the degrading messages that they are undervalued, expendable and somehow unworthy of the same successes as yourself.

You are teaching my young men to rightfully resent society.

You are teaching my young women to doubt their fortitude and their role in our community and the family unit.

You are teaching the world that the word of God is debatable –and you can choose within whom you see the face of God, and whom you do not.

You are teaching the world that your graciousness and mercifulness have prerequisites.

I encourage you to remember that one person can change the world.

I encourage you to remember that your actions and thoughts dictate our societal transformations.

I encourage you to see the human first, as we are no different than our worst perpetrator. We all are from the same Creator.

Lastly, I encourage you to remember that you too, are loved and appreciated.

Conclusion

Poverty is a pervasive, multifaceted, and indiscriminate beast that permeates neighborhoods like a plague never to be cured and often generationally shared. While poverty may display the same symptoms, the origin is vastly different depending on the demographic. Perpetuated psychological and intellectual imprisonment and oppression is often the root of misery for my families and students. This vicious cycle is not easily broken, and even for those who escape the firm grips of this plague, the ability to thrive is unlikely. There are psychological obstacles so steep, and burdens so acutely embedded that their ability to flourish without the proper supports is unreasonable. If you are doubtful, I ask you to consider for whom our country was originally designed for? What minds crafted the legal and social foundation of this country? Who created the school systems and basis for the curriculum still circulated in those schools? *The white male.* Imagine being a minority trying to navigate a society that was never designed with you in mind. You are sent into the world with preconceived notions regarding race-relations and your role in society; however, you are conflicted because you are also told by media, and those operating within these same constructs, that you are entitled to the same experiences and resources as your white counterparts. Yet, they are not accessible. The confliction begins at birth and deepens over the years as few truly consider the diabolical philosophical conception of our country's foundation. Nor is this material being presented in classrooms. Moreover, your reaction to your ever-evolving frustration is what assists in shaping your level of success –and that is fucked up.

Consider the oxymoronic paradigm of our minority politicians. While President Obama showed great leadership qualities, he was forced to uphold a constitution that was not created with him or the possibility of him in mind. He desperately wanted to institute systemic change but was not able to generate change at the foundation. Subsequently, this caused his reforms to be unsustainable. Our social systems cannot properly build upon a foundation that does not support all people. It is like raising children –if certain fundamental teachings are not given, they cannot be learned. If presented inconsistently, they project uncertainty and teach chronic skepticism. If they are presented with solidarity, the children will thrive as their roots are strong and robust enough to garner the weight of the tree in which they develop.

I invite you to seek understanding versus crafting arguments supporting your current ideologies. I charge you to observe the psychosocial discrepancies within daily human interactions between yourself and those outside of your demographic. I encourage you to familiarize yourself with the terms *assimilation* and *white privilege*. Furthermore, when you find yourself judging one's reactions or behaviors, I fervently challenge you to consider the human not solely the action displayed – remembering the origin of their present circumstance is ornately different than the majority. Lastly, study American history in its more accurate context – meaning everything you did not learn in the classroom. You should know that slavery did not instantaneously end in 1863. It took years to formally overturn. Slavery moved from the fields to the homes. Former slaves and their children became acquired *help*. This lasted for generations and still exists today. Just because there are not legal documents bonding a human to another, the psychological attachment and fear are strong enough to inhibit one's personal freedom.

Great-grandparents or even grandparents of those you know may know someone, may have worked in this capacity and/or at the bare minimum, endure racial bias daily. Our mere proximity fervidly fuels the theory that the psychological harm of discrimination directly and negatively impacts our education system and one's ability to thrive in American society. Just as bias can be passed down generationally, so can harm and fear.

You may not bear witness because you do not share this vantage point. However, it is real. It exists in the thoughts that you have while you grip your purse as you see someone approaching you on the street – someone you have been conditioned to fear. These thoughts are silent killers. They perpetuate the psychological distress and frustration, which in turn promotes incarceration and rampant recidivism rates. I am not blaming slavery for the continued social inequalities. I am blaming our inability to have meaningful, candid, challenging conversations that facilitate change. I am blaming those in power for promoting the idea that 'tradition' makes sense when our 'tradition' is serving a demographic that is barely continuing to hold the

captivity forces my students to participate in society's version of Russian roulette, and either the prison system regularly consumes the community and destroys family units, or misguided bullets steal them from us. Some of my students have been responsible for notorious crimes here in Indianapolis and are serving life sentences. They are living among death row inmates – among the walking dead –all because of a moment's decision they were not fully equipped to make.

I have visited countless homes trying to engage students in school and seeing drug paraphernalia scattered across surfaces and floors, people passed out with needles still in their arms and dogs (yes pets, true story), that were clearly intoxicated, stumbling around the home and leaning on walls to remain upright. In homes with no heat, black garbage bags covered every window, door, and human in an attempt to keep out the bitter cold. Some of my students even lived in abandoned homes. Often, the reason for not being able to attend school was to ensure the safety and livelihood of their family, Could I argue this? No –so I would bring school to them. Some qualified for homebound services, meaning a teacher could be assigned to visit the home and provide direct instruction. I offered rides to those who could not make the bus due to the responsibilities they had at home. We made it work the best we could.

That said, the system's failures were still winning. We were applying bandages to a broken levy. It was infuriating yet so deeply rooted in our soil, it felt inescapable. I recall helping students being arrested for various reasons–drugs, weapons charges, probation violations-get into the back of the Sheriff's van. I stand there with the most misunderstood young men on earth, pulling their pants up after they were thoroughly searched, tilting their chins up, telling them to keep their heads up, trying to supply them with a sliver of dignity before they were escorted to a place that would change their lives forever. It was hard to let go as I felt like I was watching them drive to the stoop of hell. They would soon be entangled in the grips of the system – further tattooed by the negative ideologies of society.

It is for these moments and these individuals that I write. Their stories should be shared –particularly with those who would never know they exist except for the media blurbs and movies. The stories presented in this book are examples of the mounting frustration of a predetermined destiny created by discrimination. This was by far the most challenging work I have authored as I am conditioned to serve first, then feel. That said, I never fully embraced the feelings behind many of my students' turmoil. This book provided the platform, and I am hopeful that your indulgence will serve as the microphone and other necessary tools to ignite this crucial and overdue conversation. The topics of race-relations and educational inequities should not be feared, instead embraced if we want to have a chance for change. Let my students and families serve as motivation –allowing their traumas, losses, and successes to become yours too.

Acknowledgements

About the
Author

Acknowledgments

I am grateful for those who supported my journey to authoring this book. Your encouragement and enthusiasm will never be forgotten. Thank you to the families in which I have been graciously accepted. You are the reason I write. You are my inspiration. Please keep your head held high, and above all else, never forget how much you are loved and appreciated.

 **Megan E. Blaising** was born and raised in Indianapolis, Indiana. She holds a Bachelor's in Social Work from Indiana University and a Master's in Applied Sociology from the University of Indianapolis. Her professional background lies in urban education – namely education reform. She has dedicated her life to fostering visibility to disenfranchised and neglected communities and advocating for quality educational opportunities for all. Megan has served in several charter and alternative educational institutions. She has served as a school counselor, social worker, legal advocate, leader, and education consultant, etc.

Currently, Megan owns and operates an educational consulting firm, Intentionality Ink, while serving as an adjunct professor at the University of Indianapolis.

CPSIA information can be obtained
at www.ICGtesting.com
Printed in the USA
BVHW032148161019
561342BV00001B/35/P

9 781732 812017